SCIENCE ESSENTIALS

WEATHER

Wonder House

WEATHER

THE CLATTER OF THE THUNDER
THE PATTER OF THE RAIN
LITTLE DROPS ON THE WINDOW PANE
IT'S MESSY BUT FUN IN RAIN

COLORFUL RAINBOW IN THE SKY
CHEERFUL BIRDS FLYING BY
THE BRIGHTLY SHINING SUN
SPRING IS SO MUCH FUN!

ORANGE, YELLOW, RED AND BROWN
IN AUTUMN LEAVES ARE FALLING DOWN
SUMMER IS HOT WITH DAYS VERY SUNNY
BEES ARE POLLINATING AND MAKING HONEY

WINTER HAS A LOT OF SNOW
LET'S HOP ON A SLEIGH AND GO
TO SEE THE DIFFERENT FACES OF WEATHER
IS FUN FOR SURE!

KATE, HOW ARE YOU DOING?
I AM FINE BOB. I AM EXCITED AS I AM PLANNING FOR MY WINTER VACATION.
IS IT WINTER THERE? WE IN SOUTH AFRICA ARE EXPERIENCING THE WET SEASON.
YES BOB. IN INDIA, IT IS THE WINTER SEASON IT IS GETTING COLDER.
OKAY, YOU CONTINUE KATE. CALL YOU LATER.
MOTHER, HOW COME IT IS WINTER IN INDIA WHILE WE ARE EXPERIENCING THE WET SEASON?
BOB, SEASONS CAN BE DIFFERENT AT DIFFERENT PLACES AROUND THE WORLD.
IT IS INFLUENCED BY A LOT OF FACTORS. BEFORE THAT LET US UNDERSTAND WHAT IS WEATHER AND CLIMATE.

WHAT IS WEATHER?
WEATHER IS THE CONDITION OF AIR AND SKY, INCLUDING WIND, TEMPERATURE, PRESSURE, HUMIDITY, ETC. WEATHER CAN BE SUNNY WITH CLEAR SKIES, COLD OR RAINY.
SUNNY
RAINY
CLOUDY
COLD
WEATHER IS DIFFERENT AT DIFFERENT PLACES AROUND THE PLANET. IN SOME PLACES, IT MAY BE SUNNY RIGHT NOW AND IN SOME PLACES, IT MAY BE CHILLY.

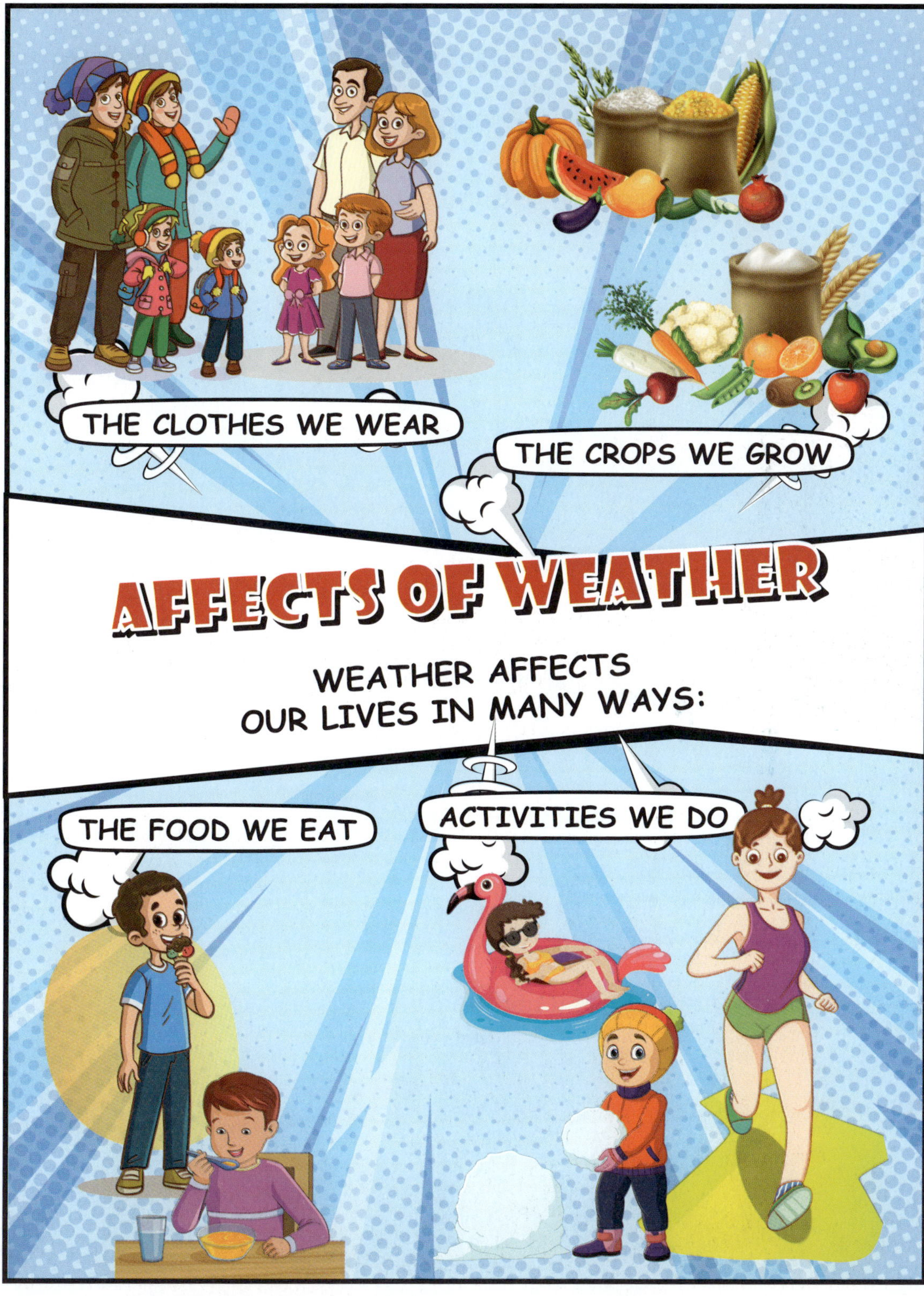
THE CLOTHES WE WEAR
THE CROPS WE GROW
AFFECTS OF WEATHER
WEATHER AFFECTS
OUR LIVES IN MANY WAYS:
THE FOOD WE EAT
ACTIVITIES WE DO

STUDY OF WEATHER

STUDYING WEATHER HELPS:
- FARMERS TO PLAN FOR THE IRRIGATION AND PROTECTION OF CROPS
- PEOPLE TO PREPARE IN ADVANCE FOR THE OUTSIDE WEATHER

WHAT CAUSES WEATHER?

THE HEAT OF THE SUN AND MOVEMENT OF THE AIR CAUSES WEATHER ON EARTH.

ELEMENTS OF WEATHER
WIND
HUMIDITY
TEMPERATURE
°C °F
LOW TEMPERATURE
HIGH TEMPERATURE
PRECIPITATION
AIR PRESSURE
ALL WEATHER ACTIVITIES HAPPEN IN THE LOWER LAYER OF THE EARTH'S ATMOSPHERE.

WIND

EARTH IS SURROUNDED BY A THICK BLANKET OF AIR CALLED ATMOSPHERE. THE SUN'S HEAT WARMS THE AIR ON EARTH. WARM AIR BEING LIGHTER RISES AND THE COLD AIR THEN RUSHES IN TO REPLACE IT. THIS MOVEMENT OF AIR IS CALLED WIND.

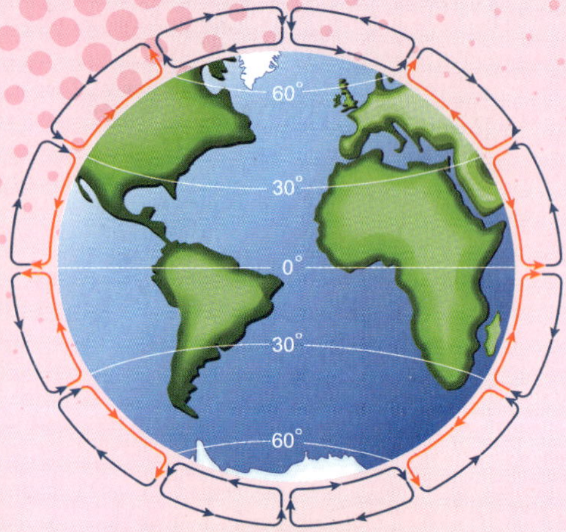

WHAT DOES WIND DO?

- BRINGS CHANGES IN THE WEATHER
- CAN BRING COOL AIR INTO WARM AREAS
- BRINGS RAIN, SNOW, DUST AND SAND

THE WINDIEST PLACE ON EARTH IS ANTARCTICA, WHERE WINDS CAN REACH UPTO THE SPEED OF 200 MILES PER HOUR.

WINDS HAVE NAMES TOO

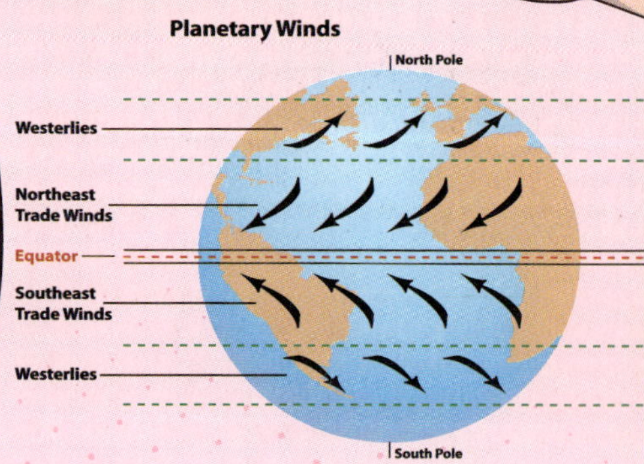

WESTERLY

WINDS ARE NAMED ACCORDING TO THE DIRECTION FROM WHICH THEY COME, NOT THE DIRECTION TOWARDS WHICH THEY BLOW. FOR INSTANCE, WIND BLOWING FROM WEST TO EAST IS CALLED WESTERLY.

MAP OF THE WINDS

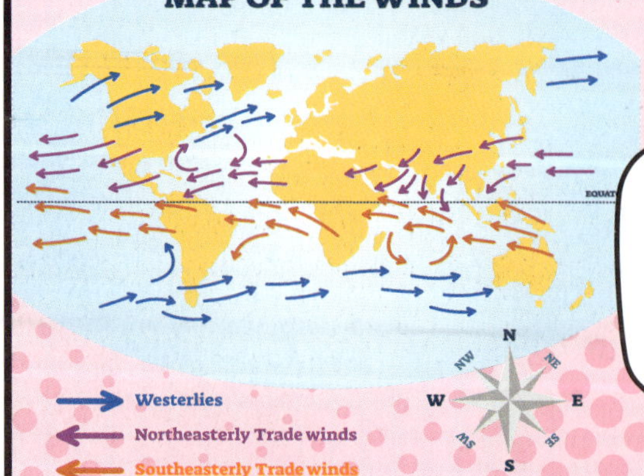

PLANETARY WINDS

PERMANENT WINDS BLOWING FROM HIGH-PRESSURE BELTS TO LOW-PRESSURE BELTS IN THE SAME DIRECTION THROUGHOUT THE YEAR ARE CALLED PLANETARY WINDS.

THE SPINNING OF EARTH CHANGES THE DIRECTION OF THE WINDS. AIR THAT MOVES TOWARDS THE EQUATOR TURNS TO THE WEST. AIR MOVING TOWARDS EARTH'S POLES TURNS TO THE EAST.
SINCE ANCIENT TIMES, PEOPLE HAVE HARNESSED THE POWER OF WIND. SAILORS DEPENDED ON THE PLANETARY WINDS TO TRAVEL ACROSS OCEANS.
THE POWER OF WIND
PEOPLE ALSO BUILT WINDMILLS TO USE WIND ENERGY TO GRIND GRAINS INTO FLOUR.
TODAY, WE USE WINDMILLS TO POWER MACHINES THAT GENERATE ELECTRICITY.

CLOUDS

CLOUDS ARE MADE UP OF MILLIONS OF TINY DROPS OF WATER FLOATING TOGETHER IN THE AIR.

THEY ARE FORMED AS A RESULT OF CONDENSATION DURING WATER CYCLE.

AIR WHEN HEATED BY THE SUN'S HEAT GETS WARM AND RISES INTO THE SKY. IT COOLS UP THERE. WATER VAPOR IN THE AIR CONDENSES (I.E. CHANGES FROM GAS TO LIQUID), INTO A GROUP OF TINY WATER DROPLETS. THIS GROUP IS WHAT WE CALL CLOUDS.

CLOUDS ARE ALL DIFFERENT!

STRATUS CLOUDS

STRATOCUMULUS CLOUDS

CUMULUS CLOUDS

CIRRUS CLOUDS

THE NAMES OF CLOUDS ARE DERIVED FROM LATIN. CIRRUS MEANS HAIR, STRATUS MEANS LAYER AND CUMULUS MEANS HEAP.

THOUGH ALL CLOUDS LOOK ALIKE, THEY ARE ACTUALLY OF DIFFERENT TYPES. THESE CLOUDS HOLD DIFFERENT AMOUNT OF WATER. THEY ARE FOUND AT DIFFERENT HEIGHTS IN THE ATMOSPHERE. THE AIR TEMPERATURE AT WHICH THEY ARE FOUND IS ALSO DIFFERENT.

PRECIPITATION
PRECIPITATION IS ALL OF THE DIFFERENT WAYS WATER FALLS FROM THE SKY.
SLEET
RAIN
SNOW
HAIL

RAIN

RAIN IS THE LIQUID FORM OF WATER THAT FALLS FROM THE SKY.

RAIN BRINGING CLOUDS APPEAR DARK AND BLACK BECAUSE THEY ARE FULL OF BIG WATER DROPLETS THAT BLOCK SUNLIGHT.

THE VAPOR RISES AND COOLS UP IN THE SKY AND CHANGES TO TINY DROPS OF WATER TO FORM CLOUDS. WHEN THE WATER DROPLETS GET BIGGER AND HEAVIER, THEY FALL ON EARTH AS RAIN.

WATER FROM SEAS, OCEANS, RIVERS, PLANTS AND LEAVES CHANGES TO WATER VAPOR DUE TO THE HEAT OF THE SUN AND EVAPORATES INTO THE AIR.

700 DRIZZLE DROPS MAKE ONE RAINDROP!

RAIN

BIG, HEAVY DROPLETS OF WATER FALLING FROM CLOUDS ARE RAIN.

DRIZZLE

VERY SMALL AND FINE DROPLETS OF WATER FALLING SLOWLY FROM LOW LEVEL CLOUDS ARE CALLED DRIZZLE.

SHOWERS

SHOWERS CAN BE EITHER SOLID OR LIQUID SUCH AS RAIN SHOWER, SNOW SHOWERS AND EVEN HAIL SHOWERS.

SNOW
CRYSTALS OF ICE FALLING ON THE EARTH ARE CALLED **SNOW**. WHEN THE TEMPERATURE IN RAIN-BEARING CLOUDS IS BELOW FREEZING POINT, WATER DROPLETS CHANGE INTO ICE CRYSTALS AND FALL AS SNOW.
AS ICE CRYSTALS FALL THEY CAN BUNDLE TOGETHER WITH OTHER ICE CRYSTALS AND FORM **SNOWFLAKES**.
SNOWFLAKES HAVE UNIQUE DESIGNS AND SHAPES. SOMETIMES, FALLING SNOWFLAKES ARE COVERED WITH THIN FILM OF WATER. THIS BINDS THEM INTO FLUFFY CLUMPS CALLED **WET SNOW**.

WHEN WEATHER GETS EXTREME

SOMETIMES, WEATHER CAN GET UNUSUALLY SEVERE IMPACTING PEOPLE AND NATURAL HABITATS. IT MAYBE SHORT-LIVED BUT CAN CAUSE EXTREME DAMAGE. HURRICANES, THUNDERSTORMS, TORNADOES, HEAT WAVES, ETC., ARE EXAMPLES OF EXTREME WEATHER.

THUNDERSTORMS

THUNDERSTORMS OCCUR WHEN LAYERS OF WARM MOIST AIR RISE TO COOLER REGIONS AND FORM SMALL WATER DROPLETS THROUGH CONDENSATION. THEY BRING HEAVY RAIN, STRONG WINDS, LIGHTNING AND SOMETIMES EVEN HAIL.

LET'S BE SAFE

LIGHTNING CAN CAUSE DAMAGE TO BUILDINGS, KILL PEOPLE AND BURN TREES! BE INDOORS DURING A THUNDERSTORM. DON'T STAND UNDER A TREE OR HOLD THINGS MADE OF METAL. STAY OUT OF WATER AND POOLS DURING A THUNDERSTORM.

HURRICANES
HURRICANES ARE VIOLENT, DESTRUCTIVE STORMS FORMED OVER THE OCEANS. THEY BRING STRONG WINDS, HEAVY RAINS, FLOODS, FROM THE OCEAN.
HURRICANES ARE CALLED CYCLONES IN THE SOUTH PACIFIC AND INDIAN OCEAN AND TYPHOONS IN THE WESTERN NORTH PACIFIC OCEAN.
VS
TORNADO
TORNADOES ARE VIOLENT, SPINNING WINDS THAT EXTEND FROM A THUNDERSTORM TO THE GROUND. THEY ARE FORMED WHEN WARM, HUMID AIR COLLIDES WITH COLD, DRY AIR.
WATERSPOUTS ARE TORNADOES FORMED OVER WATER.

BLIZZARD
A BLIZZARD IS A SNOWSTORM ACCOMPANIED WITH STRONG WINDS AND INTENSE COLD.
BLIZZARDS ARE COMMON IN VERY COLD COUNTRIES. THEY CAN BE VERY DANGEROUS DUE TO LOW VISIBILITY.
THE GREAT BLIZZARD OF 1888 IS THE MOST FAMOUS RECORDED BLIZZARD. IT OCCURRED BETWEEN MARCH 11 AND 14.
WEATHER FORECASTING
WEATHER FORECASTING MEANS KNOWING WHAT THE WEATHER IS LIKELY TO BE AT A PLACE FOR THE NEXT DAY, A FEW DAYS OR WEEKS.
PEOPLE WHO STUDY AND PREDICT WEATHER ARE CALLED METEOROLOGISTS. THEY DO THIS WITH THE HELP OF A NUMBER OF TOOLS AND WEATHER SATELLITES ORBITING THE EARTH.
THE WEATHER FORECAST
TODAY

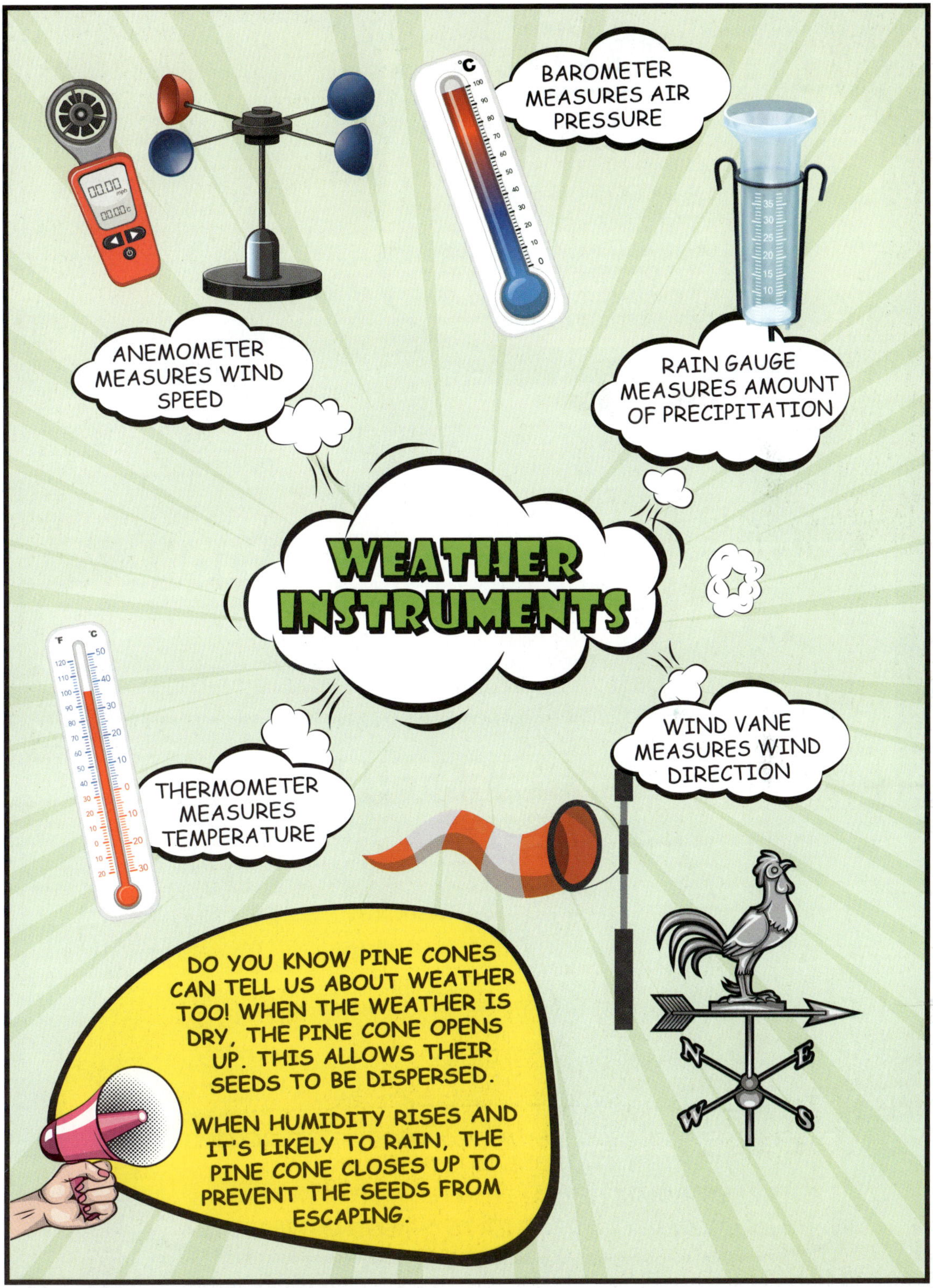
WEATHER INSTRUMENTS
ANEMOMETER MEASURES WIND SPEED
BAROMETER MEASURES AIR PRESSURE
RAIN GAUGE MEASURES AMOUNT OF PRECIPITATION
THERMOMETER MEASURES TEMPERATURE
WIND VANE MEASURES WIND DIRECTION
DO YOU KNOW PINE CONES CAN TELL US ABOUT WEATHER TOO! WHEN THE WEATHER IS DRY, THE PINE CONE OPENS UP. THIS ALLOWS THEIR SEEDS TO BE DISPERSED.
WHEN HUMIDITY RISES AND IT'S LIKELY TO RAIN, THE PINE CONE CLOSES UP TO PREVENT THE SEEDS FROM ESCAPING.

WEATHER SATELLITES

WEATHER SATELLITES ARE MAN-MADE SATELLITES THAT ARE LAUNCHED INTO THE EARTH'S ORBIT TO COLLECT WEATHER DATA FROM SPACE.

THESE SATELLITES USE SPECIAL TOOLS CALLED RADIOMETERS. THESE ARE MADE UP OF SENSORS THAT ALLOW THEM TO SCAN THE EARTH AND COLLECT INFORMATION.

GROUND STATIONS

GROUND STATIONS ARE RADIO STATIONS THAT ARE BUILT TO COLLECT DATA FROM SATELLITES. THEY ARE FOUND ALL OVER THE WORLD, ON LAND, AND EVEN IN THE MIDDLE OF THE SEA.

WEATHER MAPPING

THE DATA COLLECTED BY METEOROLOGISTS THROUGH WEATHER STATIONS IS PLOTTED ON MAPS.

EVERY FEW HOURS NEW DATA IS PLOTTED ON A NEW MAP.

THIS SHOWS HOW WEATHER IS CHANGING OVER TIME.

CLIMATE!

THE LONG TERM PATTERN OF WEATHER IN A PARTICULAR AREA IS CALLED CLIMATE. IT DESCRIBES THE AVERAGE MEASUREMENT OF TEMPERATURE, HUMIDITY, RAIN, ETC., AT A PLACE OVER THE COURSE OF YEARS.

FACTORS THAT AFFECT THE CLIMATE OF A PLACE

LATITUDE

PLACES NEAR THE EQUATOR ARE WARMER AND THOSE NEAR THE POLES ARE COLDER.

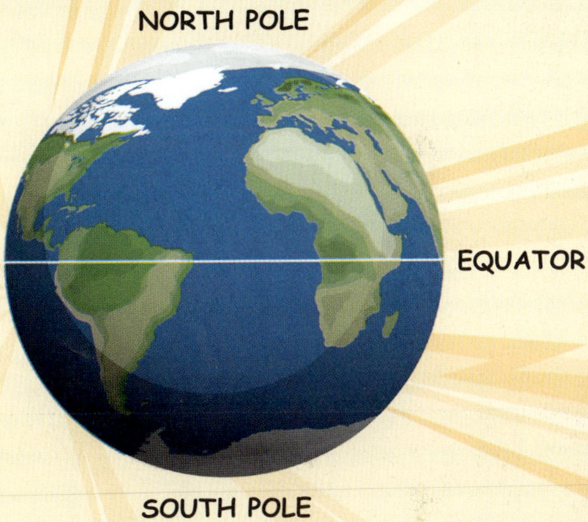

ALTITUDE

TEMPERATURE DECREASES WITH HEIGHT. HENCE, HILLY AREAS ARE COLDER THAN PLAINS.

DISTANCE FROM THE SEA
PLACES NEAR THE SEA HAVE HUMID CLIMATE AND HIGHER PRECIPITATION.
TOPOGRAPHY AND VEGETATION
THE ABUNDANCE OF PLANTS AND TYPE OF LAND IMPACTS EVAPORATION AND AMBIENT TEMPERATURE OF A PLACE. PLACES WITH MORE TREES HAVE A COOLING IMPACT ON CLIMATE.
WINDS
WINDS BRING IN HEAT/COLD FROM THE DIRECTION THEY BLOW AND THUS CHANGE THE TEMPERATURE OF A PLACE.

TYPES OF CLIMATE

THERE ARE FIVE MAIN TYPES OF CLIMATE ON EARTH.

TROPICAL
WET
MONSOON
WET AND DRY

DRY
ARID
SEMI-ARID

MILD
MEDITERRANEAN
HUMID SUBTROPICAL
MARINE

CONTINENTAL
WARM SUMMER
COOL SUMMER
SUBARCTIC

THE ATACAMA DESERT OF CHILE, SOUTH AMERICA, IS ONE OF THE DRIEST PLACES ON EARTH.

POLAR
TUNDRA
ICE CAP

SEASONS

WE HAVE FOUR MAIN SEASONS.

A SEASON IS A TIME OF THE YEAR DISTINGUISHED BY SPECIAL CLIMATE CONDITIONS. THE AMOUNT OF SUNLIGHT, TEMPERATURE, WEATHER PATTERNS ARE DIFFERENT IN EACH SEASON.

SPRING

- MORE SUNLIGHT
- TEMPERATURE BEGINS TO RISE
- DAYS GROW LONGER THAN WINTER
- TREES BLOSSOM
- HIBERNATING ANIMALS WAKE UP AND COME OUT
- MANY BIRDS AND ANIMALS RETURN FROM THEIR WINTER HOMES

SUMMER

- THE HOTTEST SEASON OF THE YEAR
- DAYS ARE LONGER AND NIGHTS SHORTER
- TREES ARE FULL OF LEAVES
- MANY TREES AND PLANTS BEAR FRUITS
- AREAS AROUND THE NORTH AND SOUTH POLES HAVE CONSTANT SUNLIGHT EVEN AT MIDNIGHT BECAUSE THE SUN DOES NOT SET

AUTUMN
• DAYS GET SHORTER
• TEMPERATURE BEGINS TO DROP
• LEAVES TURN INTO SHADES OF RED, ORANGE, BROWN AND YELLOW
• DECIDUOUS TREES SHED THEIR LEAVES
• MANY PLANTS MAKE SEEDS
• SOME ANIMALS PREPARE FOR WINTERS BY GROWING THICKER FUR OR BY GAINING WEIGHT
WINTER
• THE COLDEST SEASON OF THE YEAR
• DAYS ARE SHORT AND NIGHTS ARE LONG
• TREES SURVIVE BY LOSING THEIR LEAVES
• MANY ANIMALS GO FOR A DEEP SLEEP CALLED HIBERNATION
• SOME ANIMALS MOVE TO WARMER PLACES
• AREAS AROUND THE NORTH AND SOUTH POLES ARE COMPLETELY DARK BECAUSE THE SUN DOES NOT RISE

CLIMATE CHANGE

LONG TERM SHIFTS IN TEMPERATURE AND WEATHER PATTERNS OF A PLACE REFERS TO CLIMATE CHANGE.

OVER THE YEARS, MANY HUMAN ACTIVITIES HAVE BEEN THE CAUSE OF CLIMATE CHANGE. THESE ARE:

- BURNING FOSSIL FUELS
- CLEARING LAND AND FORESTS
- LANDFILLS FOR GARBAGE
- GREENHOUSE EMISSIONS FROM INDUSTRIES AND TRANSPORT

CONSEQUENCES OF CLIMATE CHANGE

- INTENSE DROUGHTS
- WATER SCARCITY
- FOREST FIRES
- RISING SEA LEVELS
- FLOODS
- MELTING POLAR ICE
- CATASTROPHIC STORMS
- DECLINING BIODIVERSITY

WHAT WE CAN DO?

- SWITCHING TO RENEWABLE SOURCES OF ENERGY
- SAVE ENERGY AT HOME
- WALK, CYCLE OR USE PUBLIC TRANSPORT
- FOLLOW THE THREE R's—REDUCE, REUSE AND RECYCLE
- USE NATURAL RESOURCES, ELECTRICITY AND WATER WISELY